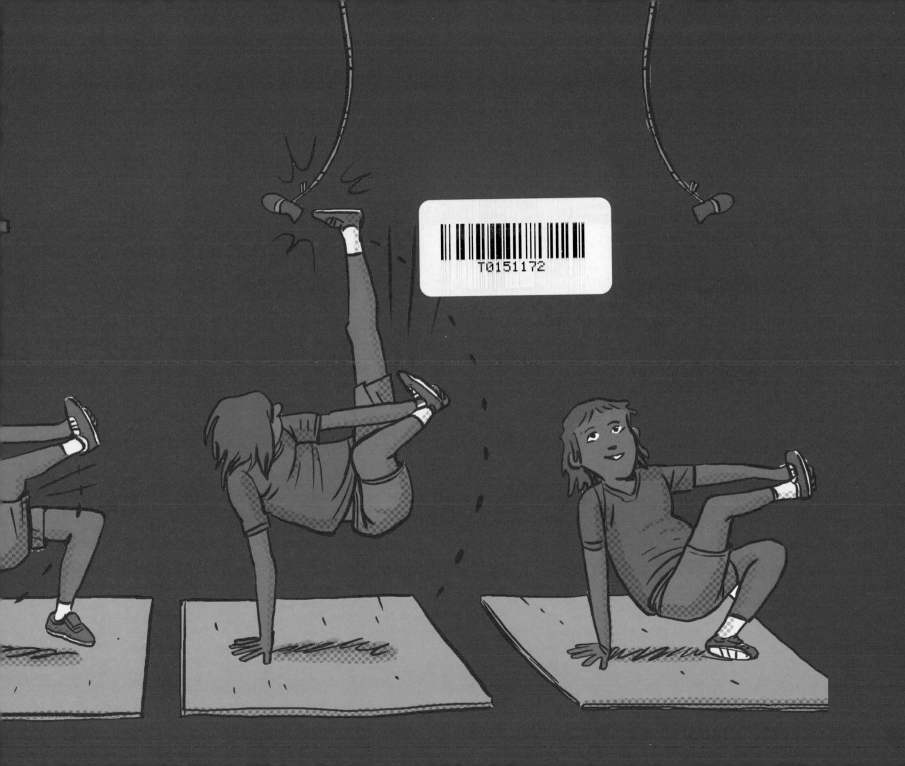

INUIT GAMES

The Nunavummi reading series is a Nunavut-developed levelled book series that supports literacy development while teaching readers about the people, traditions, and environment of the Canadian Arctic.

Nunavummi

Published in Canada by Nunavummi, an imprint of
Inhabit Education Books Inc. | www.inhabiteducation.com

Inhabit Education Books Inc.
(Iqaluit) P.O. Box 2129, Iqaluit, Nunavut, X0A 1H0
(Toronto) 191 Eglinton Avenue East, Suite 301, Toronto, Ontario, M4P 1K1

Printed in Canada.

ISBN: 978-1-77450-175-7

INHABIT
EDUCATION

INUIT GAMES

WRITTEN BY
Thomas Anguti Johnston

ILLUSTRATED BY
Sigmundur Thorgeirsson

Do you know anyone who plays Inuit games?

Inuit games have been played as long as anyone can remember. They are played for fun and to help build survival skills. Inuit games are played all over the Arctic!

People have always played Inuit games for fun. Inuit games are also an important way for people to stay healthy and strong for life in the Arctic.

Inuit games can test people's toughness and flexibility. Inuit games also help strengthen the body and the mind. These are all things that hunters need to stay strong and help feed their communities.

6

People play Inuit games at school, at festivals, and at tournaments.

During tournaments, players come from all over to play against each other. Tournaments are a lot of fun. The players always show respect and have a good time.

There are many different kinds of Inuit games. Different games test different skills. For example, some games are played to see who has stronger arms. Some games test who can jump farther or kick higher.

So, what are some of these games?

Strength Games

Strength games are usually played by two people. They are also called muscle games.

Strength games keep hunters strong and healthy even when they can't go hunting. Hunters sometimes can't go hunting because they have to wait for the ice to freeze or a storm to pass.

Here are some popular strength games.

In arm pull, two players see who has stronger arms. They hook their arms together and try to pull each other over.

In leg wrestling, two players see who has stronger legs. They lie on their backs and each use one leg to try to push the other player's leg down.

In muskox push, the two players are on all fours, like a muskox! They push hard against each other with their shoulders.

In head pull, the players put one band around both of their heads. Then each player tries to pull the other using only his or her head and neck.

Kicking Games

Kicking games test the players' flexibility and balance.

Kicking games are played with a kickstand. A kickstand is a piece of equipment that you can hang a target from. The target is called a *nattinnguaq*, or seal target. That's because it is made out of sealskin.

A popular kicking game is the one-foot high kick. Players see who can jump and kick the highest.

Each player jumps off the ground with both feet. Then the player has to kick the target with one foot and land on that same foot. That's the tricky part!

In some kicking games, the player has to stay partly on the ground during the kick. One of these games is called the Alaskan high kick. This game is difficult and takes a lot of practice. But it is also a lot of fun!

21

In the Alaskan high kick, the player sits under the target with one hand on the ground. The other hand holds the opposite foot. Then the player uses the free foot to kick the target.

The player must start and land in the same position and keep one hand on the ground the whole time!

Long ago, Inuit games were played outside on the land. Today, we play them in gyms.

It is important to keep playing these games and passing them on. The best lesson you can learn from Inuit games is to have fun playing with friends and family.

Nunavummi
Reading Series

The Nunavummi reading series is a Nunavut-developed levelled book series that supports literacy development while teaching readers about the people, traditions, and environment of the Canadian Arctic.

Level 10
- 16–32 pages
- Sentences and stories become longer and more complex
- Varied punctuation
- Dialogue is included in fiction texts
- Readers rely more on the words than the images to decode the text

11
- 24–32 pages
- Sentences become complex and varied
- Varied punctuation
- Dialogue is included in fiction texts and is necessary to understand the story
- Readers rely more on the words than the images to decode the text

Level 12
- 24–40 pages
- Sentences are complex and vary in length
- Lots of varied punctuation
- Dialogue is included in fiction texts and is necessary to understand the story
- Readers rely on the words to decode the text; images are present but only somewhat supportive

Fountas & Pinnell Text Level: L

This book has been officially levelled using the F&P Text Level Gradient™ Leveling System.

Thomas Anguti Johnston

 Thomas Anguti Johnston grew up moving around the Baffin region of Nunavut and northern Quebec (Nunavik). He now lives in Iqaluit, Nunavut, with his two daughters, Amy and Leah, and his partner, Aqattuaq. Anguti has been involved in the Inuit political realm, with the National Inuit Youth Council and Inuit Tapiriit Kanatami. He decided to pursue his passion of filmmaking and writing full-time in 2014 and hasn't looked back. Anguti has received the Nunavut Commissioner's award for youth development and the Diamond Jubilee award for media arts. Anguti is an actor, writer, and film director with a passion for telling Inuit stories.

Sigmundur Thorgeirsson

Sigmundur Thorgeirsson is an Icelandic illustrator living in Toronto. He studied drawing at The Reykjavik School of Visual Arts in Iceland and then illustration with an emphasis on entertainment at Laguna College of Art and Design in California, USA. When not illustrating books he can be found making indie games and picking up his dog's poop.

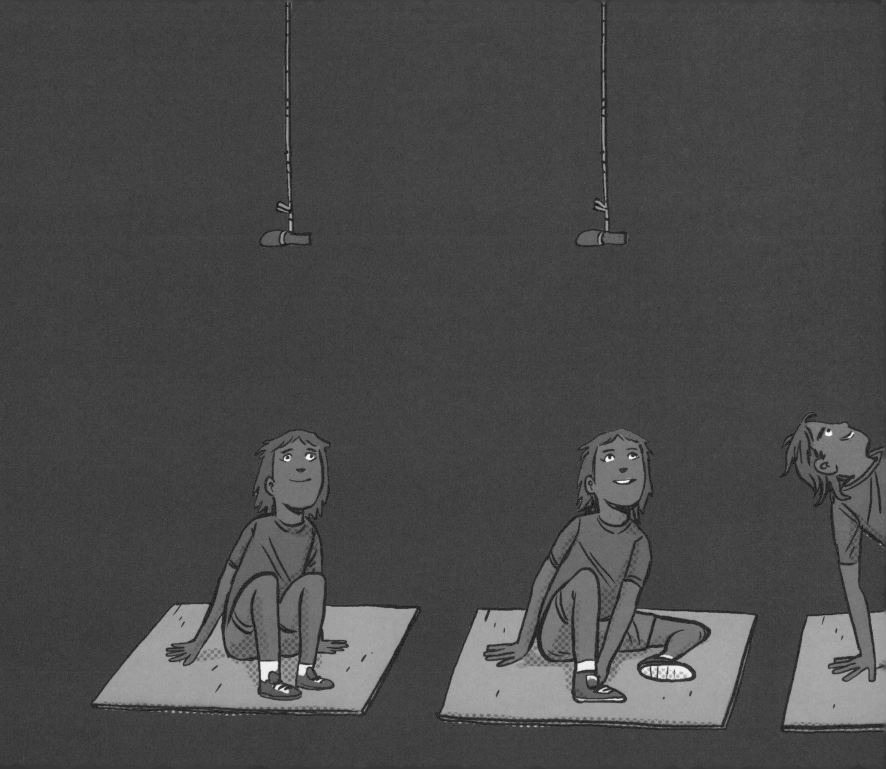